The Holy Science

SRI YUKTESWAR GIRI

First published 1894
Translated from the 1949 Edition

TABLE OF CONTENTS

May you find this book spiritually Motivating LOVE Nachi

INTRODUCTION

This Kaivalya Darsanam (exposition of Final Truth) has been written by Priya Nath Swami, son of Kshetranath and Kaciambini of the Karar family.

At the request in Allahabad of the Great Preceptor (Mahavatar Babaji) near the end of the 194th year of the present Dwapara Yuga, this exposition has been published for the benefit of the world.

The purpose of this book is to show as clearly as possible that there is an essential unity in all religions; that there is no difference in the truths inculcated by the various faiths; that there is but one method by which the world, both external and internal, has evolved; and that there is but one Goal admitted by all scriptures. But this basic truth is one not easily comprehended. The discord existing between the different religions, and the ignorance of men, make it almost impossible to lift the veil and have a look at this grand verity. The creeds foster a spirit of hostility and dissension; ignorance widens the gulf that separates one creed from another. Only a few specially gifted persons can rise superior to the influence of their professed creeds and find absolute unanimity in the truths propagated by all great faiths.

The object of this book is to point out the harmony underlying the various religions, and to help in binding them together. This task is indeed a herculean one, but at Allahabad I was entrusted with the mission by a holy command. Allahabad, the sacred Prayaga Tirtha, the place of confluence of the Ganges, Jamuna, and Saraswati rivers, is a site for the congregation of worldly men and of spiritual devotees at the time of Kumbha Mela. Worldly men cannot transcend the

3

mundane limit in which they have confined themselves; nor can spiritual devotees, having once renounced the world, deign to come down and mix themselves in its turmoil. Yet men who are wholly engrossed in earthly concerns stand in definite need of help and guidance from those holy beings who bring light to the race. So a place there must be where union between the two sets is possible. Tirtha affords such a meeting place. Situated as it is on the beach of the world, storms and buffets touch it not; the sadhus (ascetics) with a message for the benefit of humanity find a Kumbha Mela to be an ideal place to impart instruction to those who can heed it.

A message of such a nature was I chosen to propagate when I paid a visit to the Kumbha Mela being held at Allahabad in January 1894. As I was walking along the bank of the Ganges, I was summoned by a man and was afterwards honored by an interview with a great holy person, Babaji, the gurudeva of my own guru, Lahiri Mahasaya, of Banaras. This holy personage at the Kumba Mela was thus my own paramguruji maharaj [the guru of one's guru], though this was our first meeting.

During my conversation with Babaji, we spoke of the particular class of men who now frequent these places of pilgrimage. I humbly suggested that there were men greater by far in intelligence than most of those then present, men living in distant parts of the world — Europe and America — professing different creeds, and ignorant of the real significance of the Kumbha Mela. They were men fit to hold communion with the spiritual devotees, so far as intelligence is concerned; yet such intellectual men in foreign lands were, alas, wedded in many cases to rank materialism. Some of them, though famous for their investigations in the realms of science and philosophy, do not recognize the essential unity in religion. The professed creeds serve as nearly insurmountable barriers that threaten to separate mankind forever.

My paramguruji maharaj Babaji smiled and, honoring me with the title of Swami, imposed on me the task of this book. I was chosen, I do not know the reason why, to remove the barriers and to help in establishing the basic truth in all religions.

The book is divided into four sections, according to the four stages in the development of knowledge. The highest aim of religion is Atmajnanam, Self-knowledge. But to attain this, knowledge of the external world is necessary. Therefore the first section of the book deals with Veda, the gospel, and seeks to establish fundamental truths of creation and to describe the evolution and involution of the world.

All creatures, from the highest to the lowest in the link of creation, are found eager to realize three things: Existence, Consciousness, and Bliss. These purposes or goals are the subject for discussion in the second section of the book. The third section deals with the method of realizing the three purposes of life. The fourth section discusses the revelations which come to those who have traveled far to realize the three ideals of life and who are very near their destination.

The method I have adopted in the book is first to enunciate a proposition in Sanskrit terms of the Oriental sages, and then to explain it by reference to the holy scriptures of the West. In this way I have tried my best to show that there is no real discrepancy, much less any real conflict, between the teachings of the East and the West. Written as the book is, under the inspiration of my paramgurudeva, and in a Dwapara Age of rapid development in all departments of knowledge, I hope that [the significance of the book will not be missed by those for whom it is meant.] ∞

A short discussion with mathematical calculation of the yugas or ages will explain the fact that the present age for the world is Dwapara Yuga, and that 194 years of the Yuga have now (a.d. 1894) passed away, bringing a rapid development in man's knowledge.

We learn from Oriental astronomy that moons revolve around their planets, and planets turning on their axes revolve with their moons round the sun; and the sun, with its planets and their moons, takes some star for its dual and revolves round it in about 24,000 years of our earth — a celestial phenomenon which causes the backward movement of the equinoctial points around the zodiac. The sun also has another motion by which it revolves round a grand center called Vishnunabhi, ↴ *navel* which is the seat of the creative power, Brahma, the *center* universal magnetism. Brahma regulates dharma, the *of* mental virtue of the internal world. *the universe*

When the sun in its revolution round its dual comes to the place nearest to this grand center, the seat of Brahma (an event which takes place when the Autumnal Equinox comes to the first point of Aries), dharma, the mental virtue, becomes so much developed that man can easily comprehend all, even the mysteries of Spirit.

The Autumnal Equinox will be falling, at the beginning of the twentieth century, among the fixed stars of the Virgo constellation, and in the early part of the Ascending Dwapara Yuga.

After 12,000 years, when the sun goes to the place in its orbit which is farthest from Brahma, the grand center (an event which takes place when the Autumnal Equinox is on the first point of Libra), dharma, the mental virtue, comes to such a reduced state that man cannot grasp anything beyond the gross material creation. Again, in the same manner, when the sun in its course of revolution begins to advance toward the place nearest to the grand center, dharma, the mental virtue, begins to develop; this growth is gradually completed in another 12,000 years.

Each of these periods of 12,000 years brings a complete change, both externally in the material world, and internally in the intellectual or electric world, and is called one of the Daiva Yugas or Electric Couple. Thus, in a period of 24,000 years, the sun completes the revolution around its dual and finishes one electric cycle consisting of 12,000 years in an ascending arc and 12,000 years in a descending arc.

Development of dharma, the mental virtue, is but gradual and is divided into four different stages in a period of 12,000 years. The time of 1200 years during which the sun passes through a 1/20th portion of its orbit is called Kali Yuga. Dharma, the mental virtue, is then in its first stage and is only a quarter developed; the human intellect cannot comprehend anything beyond the gross material of this ever-changing creation, the external world.

The period of 2400 years during which the sun passes through the 2/20th portion of its orbit is called Dwapara Yuga. Dharma, the mental virtue, is then in the second stage of development and is but half complete; the human intellect can then comprehend the fine

7

matters or electricities and their attributes which are the creating principles of the external world.

The period of 3600 years during which the sun passes through the 3/20th part of its orbit is called Treta Yuga. Dharma, the mental virtue, is then in the third stage; the human intellect becomes able to comprehend the divine magnetism, the source of all electrical forces on which the creation depends for its existence.

The period of 4800 years during which the sun passes through the remaining 4/20th portion of its orbit is called Satya Yuga. Dharma, the mental virtue, is then in its fourth stage and completes its full development; the human intellect can comprehend all, even God the Spirit beyond this visible world.

Manu, a great rishi (illumined sage) of Satya Yuga, describes these Yugas more clearly in the following passage from his Samhita:

"Four thousands of years, they say, is the Krita Yuga (Satya Yuga or the "Golden Age" of the world). Its morning twilight has just as many hundreds, and its period of evening dusk is of the same length (i.e., 400+4000 + 400=4800). In the other three ages, with their morning and evening twilights, the thousands and the hundreds decrease by one (i.e., 300 + 3000 + 300 = 3600; etc.). That fourfold cycle comprising 12,000 years is called an Age of the Gods. The sum of a thousand divine ages constitutes one day of Brahma; and of the same length is its night."

The period of Satya Yuga is 4000 years in duration; 400 years before and after Satya Yuga proper are its sandhis or periods of mutation with the preceding and the succeeding Yugas respectively; hence 4800 years in all is the proper age of Satya Yuga. In the calculation of the period of other Yugas and Yugasandhis, it is laid down that the numeral one should be deducted from the numbers of both thousands and hundreds which indicate the periods of the previous Yugas and sandhis. From this rule it appears that 3000 years is the length of Treta Yuga, and 300 years before and after are its sandhis, the periods of mutation, which make a total of 3600 years.

So 2000 years is the age of Dwapara Yuga, with 200 years before and after as its sandhis; a total of 2400 years. Lastly, 1000 years is the length of Kali Yuga, with 100 years before and after as its sandhis; a total of 1200 years. Thus 12,000 years, the sum total of all periods of these four Yugas, is the length of one of the Daiva Yugas or Electric Couple, two of which, that is, 24,000 years, make the electric cycle complete.

From 1 1,501 B.C., when the Autumnal Equinox was on the first point of Aries, the sun began to move away from the point of its orbit nearest to the grand center toward the point farthest from it, and accordingly the intellectual power of man began to diminish. During the 4800 years which the sun took to pass through one of the Satya Couples or 4/20th part of its orbit, the intellect of man lost altogether the power of grasping spiritual knowledge. During the 3600 years following, which the sun look to pass through the Descending Treta Yuga, the intellect gradually lost all power of grasping the knowledge of divine magnetism. During the 2400 years next following, while the sun passed through the Descending Dwapara Yuga, the human intellect lost its power of grasping the knowledge of electricities and their attributes. In 1200 more years the sun passed through the Descending Kali Yuga and reached the point in its orbit which is farthest from the grand center; the Autumnal Equinox was on the first point of Libra. The intellectual power of man was so much diminished that it could no longer comprehend anything beyond the gross material of creation. The period around a.d. 500 was thus the darkest part of Kali Yuga and of the whole cycle of 24,000 years. History indeed bears out the accuracy of these ancient calculations of the Indian rishis, and records the widespread ignorance and suffering in all nations at that period.

From a.d. 499 onward, the sun began to advance toward the grand center, and the intellect of man started gradually to develop. During the 1100 years of the Ascending Kali Yuga, which brings us to a.d. 1599, the human intellect was so dense that it could not comprehend the electricities, Sukshmabhuta, the fine matters of creation. In the political world also, generally speaking, there was no peace in any kingdom.

Subsequent to this period, when the 100-year transitional sandhi of Kali Yuga set in, to effect a union with the following Dwapara Yuga, men began to notice the existence of fine matters, panchatanmatra or the attributes of electricities; and political peace began to be established.

About a.d. 1600, William Gilbert discovered magnetic forces and observed the presence of electricity in all material substances. In 1609 Kepler discovered important laws of astronomy, and Galileo produced a telescope. In 1621 Drebbel of Holland invented the microscope. About 1670 Newton discovered the law of gravitation. In 1700 Thomas Savery made use of a steam engine in raising water. Twenty years later Stephen Gray discovered the action of electricity on the human body.

In the political world, people began to have respect for themselves, and civilization advanced in many ways. England united with Scotland and became a powerful kingdom. Napoleon Bonaparte introduced his new legal code into southern Europe. America won its independence, and many parts of Europe were peaceful.

With the advance of science, the world began to be covered with railways and telegraphic wires. By the help of steam engines, electric machines, brought into practical use, although their nature was not clearly understood. In 1899, on completion of the period of 200 years of Dwapara Sandhi, the time of mutation, the true Dwapara Yuga of 2000 years will commence and will give to mankind in general a thorough understanding of the electricities and their attributes.

Such is the great influence of Time which governs the universe. No man can overcome this influence except him who, blessed with pure love, the heavenly gift of nature, becomes divine; being baptized in the sacred stream Prancwa (the holy Om vibration), he comprehends the Kingdom of God.

The position of the world in the Dwapara Sandhi era at present (a.d. 1894) is not correctly shown in the Hindu almanacs. The astronomers and astrologers who calculate the almanacs have been guided by wrong annotations of certain Sanskrit scholars (such as Kulluka Bhatta) of the dark age of Kali Yuga, and now maintain that the length of Kali Yuga is 432,000 years, of which 4994 have (in a.d. 1894) passed away, leaving 427,006 years still remaining. A dark prospect! and fortunately one not true.

The mistake crept into almanacs for the first time about 700 b.c. during the reign of Raja Parikshit, just after the completion of the last Descending Dwapara Yuga. At that time Maharaja Yudhisthira, noticing the appearance of the dark Kali Yuga, made over his throne to his grandson, the said Raja Parikshit. Maharaja Yudhisthira, together with all the wise men of his court, retired to the Himalaya Mountains, the paradise of the world. Thus there was none in the court of Raja Parikshit who could understand the principle of correctly calculating the ages of the several Yugas.

Hence, after the completion of the 2400 years of the then current Dwapara Yuga, no one dared to make the introduction of the dark Kali Yuga more manifest by beginning to calculate from its first year and to put an end to the number of Dwapara years.

According to this wrong method of calculation, therefore, the first year of Kali Yuga was numbered 2401 along with the age of Dwapara Yuga. In a.d. 499, when 1200 years, the length of the true Kali Yuga, was complete, and the sun had reached the point of its orbit farthest from the grand center (when the Autumnal Equinox was on the first point of Libra in the heavens), the age of Kali in its darkest period was then numbered by 3600 years instead of by 1200.

With the commencement of the Ascending Kali Yuga, after a.d. 499, the sun began to advance in its orbit nearer to the grand center, and accordingly the intellectual power of man started to develop. Therefore the mistake in the almanacs began to be noticed by the wise men of the time, who found that the calculations of the ancient rishis had fixed the period of one Kali Yuga at 1 200 years only. But as the intellect of these wise men was not yet suitably developed, they could make out only the mistake itself, and not the reason for it. By way of reconciliation, they fancied that 1200 years, the real age of Kali, were not the ordinary years of our earth, but were so many daiva years ("years of the gods"), consisting of 1 2 daiva months of 30 daiva days each, with each daiva day being equal to one ordinary solar year of our earth. Hence according to these men 1200 years of Kali Yuga must be equal to 432,000 years of our earth.

In coming to a right conclusion, however, we should take into consideration the position of the Vernal Equinox at spring in the year 1894.

The astronomical reference books show the Vernal Equinox now to be 20°54'36" distant from the first point of Aries (the fixed star Revati), and by calculation it will appear that 1394 years have passed since the time when the Vernal Equinox began to recede from the first point of Aries.

Deducting 1200 years (the length of the last Ascending Kali Yuga) from 1394 years, we get 194 to indicate the present year of the world's entrance into the Ascending Dwapara Yuga. The mistake of older almanacs will thus be clearly explained when we add 3600 years to this period of 1394 years and get 4994 years — which according to the prevailing mistaken theory represents the present year (a.d. 1894) in the Hindu almanacs.

In this book certain truths such as those about the properties of magnetism, its auras, different sorts of electricities, etc., have been mentioned, although modern science has not yet fully discovered them. The five sorts of electricity can be easily understood if one will direct his attention to the nerve properties, which are purely electrical in nature. Each of the five sensory nerves has its characteristic and unique function to perform. The optic nerve carries light and does not perform the functions of the auditory and other nerves; the auditory nerve in its turn carries sound only, without performing the functions of any other nerves, and so on. Thus it is clear that there are five sorts of electricity, corresponding to the five properties of cosmic electricity.

So far as magnetic properties are concerned, the grasping power of the human intellect is at present so limited that it would be quite useless to attempt to make the matter understood by the general public. The intellect of man in Treta Yuga will comprehend the attributes of divine magnetism (the next Treta Yuga will start in a.d. 4099). There are indeed exceptional personages now living who, having overcome the influence of Time, can grasp today what ordinary people cannot grasp; but this book is not for those exalted ones, who require nothing of it.

In concluding this introduction, we may observe that the different planets, exercising their influence over the various days of the week, have lent their names to their respective days; similarly, the different constellations of stars, having influence over various months, have lent their names to the Hindu months. Each of the great Yugas has much influence over the period of time covered by it; hence, in designating the years it is desirable that such terms should indicate to which Yuga they belong.

As the Yugas are calculated from the position of the equinox, the method of numbering the years in reference to their respective Yuga is based on a scientific principle; its use will obviate much inconvenience which has arisen in the past owing to association of the various eras with persons of eminence rather than with celestial phenomena of the fixed stars. We therefore propose to name and number the year in which this introduction has been written as 194 Dwapara, instead of a.d. 1894, to show the exact time of the Yuga now passing. This method of calculation was prevalent in India till the reign of Raja Vikramaditya, when the Samvat era was introduced. As the Yuga method of calculation recommends itself to reason, we follow it, and recommend that it be followed by the public in general.

Now, in this 194th year of Dwapara Yuga, the dark age of Kali having long since passed, the world is reaching out for spiritual knowledge, and men require loving help one from the other. The publishing of this book, requested from me by my holy paramguru maharaj Babaji, will, I hope, be of spiritual service.

-Swami Sri Yukteswar Giri
Serampore, West Bengal
The 26th Falgun, 194 Dwapara (a.d. 1894)

CHAPTER 1
THE GOSPEL

> SUTRA 1: "Parambrahma (Spirit or God) is infinite, complete, without start or end. It is one, undividable Being."

The Eternal Father, God, Swami Parambrahma, is the only Real Substance, Sat, and is all in all in the universe.

Why God is not comprehensible:
Man possesses eternal faith and believes intuitively in the existence of a Substance, of which the objects of sense — sound, touch, sight, taste, and smell, the component parts of this visible world — are but properties. As man identifies himself with his material body, composed of the aforesaid properties, he is able to comprehend by these imperfect organs these properties only, and not the Substance to which these properties belong. The Eternal Father, God, the only Substance in the universe, is therefore not comprehensible by man of this material world, unless he becomes divine by lifting his self above this creation of Darkness or Maya. See Hebrews 11:1 and John 8:28.

"Now faith is the substance of things hoped for, the evidence of things not seen. "

"Then said Jesus unto them, When ye have lifted up the son of man, then shall ye know that I am he."

> SUTRA 2: "In Parambrahma is the source of all knowing and love, the root of all power and joy."

Prakriti or Nature of God. The Almighty Force, Sakti, or in other words the Eternal Joy, Anayida, which produced the world; and the Omniscient feeling, Chit, which makes this world conscious, demonstrate the Nature, Prakriti, of God the Father.

How God is comprehended. As man is the likeness of God, directing his attention inward he can comprehend within him the said Force and Feeling, the sole properties of his Self — the Force Almighty as his will, Vasana, with enjoyment, Bhoga; and the Feeling Omniscient as his Consciousness, Chetana, that enjoys, Bhokta. See Genesis 1 :27.

"So God created man in his own image, in the image of God created he him; male and female created he them."

> SUTRA 3: "Parambrahma emanates creation, inert Nature (Prakriti), to emerge. From Om (Pranava, the Word, the manifestation of the Omnipotent Force), come Kala, Time; Desa, Space; and Anu, the Atom (the vibratory structure of creation)."

The Word, Amen (Om), is the beginning of the Creation. The manifestation of Omnipotent Force (the Repulsion and its complementary expression, Omniscient Feeling or Love, the Attraction) is vibration, which appears as a peculiar sound: the Word, Amen, Aurn. In its different aspects Om presents the idea of change, which is Time, Kala, in the Ever-Unchangeable; and the idea of division, which is Space, Desa, in the Ever- Indivisible.

The Four Ideas: the Word, Time, Space, and the Atom. The ensuing effect is the idea of particles— the innumerable atoms, pair a or anu. These four — the Word, Time, Space, and the Atom — are therefore one and the same, and substantially nothing but mere ideas.

This manifestation of the Word (becoming flesh, the external material) created this visible world. So the Word, Amen, Om, being the manifestation of the Eternal Nature of the Almighty Father or His Own Self, is inseparable from and nothing but God Himself; as the burning power is inseparable from and nothing but the fire itself. See Revelation 3:14; John 1:1,3,14.

"These things saith the Amen, the faithful and true witness, the beginning of the creation of God. "

"In the beginning was the Word, and the Word was with God, and the Word was God. . . .All things were made by him; and without him was not anything made that was made And the Word was made flesh and dwelt among us. "

> SUTRA 4: "The fundament of creation is Anu or the Atoms. Together they are called Maya or the Lord's veil of projection; each individual Anu is called Avidya, Ignorance."

Atoms the throne of Spirit the Creator. These Atoms, which represent within and without the four ideas mentioned above, are the throne of Spirit, the Creator, which shining on them creates this universe. They are called en masse Maya, the Darkness, as they keep the Spiritual Light out of comprehension; and each of them separately is called Avidya, the Ignorance, as it makes man ignorant even of his own Self. Hence the aforesaid four ideas which give rise to ail those confusions are mentioned in the Bible as so many beasts. Man, so long as he identifies himself with his gross material body, holds a position far inferior to that of the primal fourfold Atom and necessarily fails to comprehend the same. But when he raises himself to the level thereof, he not only comprehends this Atom, both inside and outside, but also the whole creation, both unmanifested and manifested (i.e., "before and behind"). See Revelation 4:6.

"And in the midst of the throne, and round about the throne, were four beasts full of eyes before and behind. "

> SUTRA 5: "The Omniscient Love aspect of Parambrahma is Kutastha Chaitanya. The individual Self, being Its manifestation, is one with It."

Kutastha Chaitanya, the Holy Ghost, Purushottama The manifestation of Premabijam Chit (Attraction, the Omniscient Love) is Life, the Omnipresent Holy Spirit, and is called the Holy Ghost, Kutastha Chaiianya or Purushottama, which shines on the Darkness, Maya, to attract every portion of it toward Divinity. But the Darkness, Maya, or its individual parts,* Avidya the Ignorance, being repulsion itself, cannot receive or comprehend the Spiritual Light, but reflects it.

Abhasa Chaiianya or Purusha, the Sons of God.

This Holy Ghost, being the manifestation of the Omniscient Nature of the Eternal Father, God, is no other substance than God Himself; and so these reflections of spiritual rays are called the Sons of God — Abhasa Chaiianya or Purusha, See John 1:4,5, 11.

"In him was life; and the life was the light of men. And the light shineth in darkness; and the darkness comprehended it not."

"He came unto his own, and his own received him not."

SUTRA 6: "The Atom, under the influence of Chit (universal knowledge) forms the Chitta or the Consciousness of mind, which when spiritualized is called Buddhi, Intelligence. Its opposite is Manas, Mind, in which lives the self with Ahamkara, Ego, the idea of separate existence."

Chitta, the Heart; Ahamkara, Ego, the son of man. This Atom, Avidya, the Ignorance, being under the influence of Universal Love, Chit, the Holy Spirit, becomes spiritualized, like iron filings in a magnetic aura, and possessed of consciousness, the power of feeling, when it is called Mahal, the Heart, Chitta; and being such, the idea of separate existence of self appears in it, which is called Ahamkara, Ego, the son of man.

Buddhi, the Intelligence; Manas, the Mind. Being thus magnetized, it has two poles, one of which attracts it toward the Real Substance, Sat, and the other repels it from the same. The former is called Sattwa or Buddhi, the Intelligence, which determines what is Truth; and the latter, being a particle of Repulsion, the Almighty Force spiritualized as aforesaid, produces the ideal world for enjoyment (ananda) and is called Anandatwa or Manas, the Mind.

SUTRAS 7-10: "Chitta, the spiritualized Atom, in which Ahamkara (the idea of separate existence of Self) appears, has five manifestations (aura electricities).
They (the five aura electricities) constitute the causal body of Purusha.
The five electricities, Pancha Tattwa, from their three attributes, Gunas — Sattwa (positive), Rajas (neutralizing), and Tamas (negative)- — produce Jnanandriyas (organs of sense),

Karmendriyas (organs of action), and Tanmatras (objects of sense).
These fifteen attributes plus Mind and Intelligence constitute the seventeen 'fine limbs' of the subtle body, the Lingasarira."

Pancha Tattwa, the Root-Causes of creation, are the causal body. This spiritualized Atom, Chitta (the Heart), being the Repulsion manifested, produces five sorts of aura electricities from its five different parts: one from the middle, two from the two extremities, and the other two from the spaces intervening between the middle and each of the extremities. These five sorts of electricities, being attracted under the influence of Universal Love (the Holy Ghost) toward the Real Substance, Sat, produce a magnetic field which is called the body of Sattw a Biiddhi, the Intelligence. These five electricities being the causes of all other creations are called Pancha Tattwa, the five Root-Causes, and are considered the causal body of Purusha, the Son of God, Three Gunas, the electric attributes. The electricities, being evolved from the polarized Chitta, are also in a polarized state and are endowed with its three attributes or Gunas: Sattiva the positive, Tamos the negative, and Rajas the neutralizing.

Jnanendriyas, the five organs of the senses. The positive attributes of the five electricities are Jnanendriyas, the organs of the senses — smell, taste, sight, touch, and hearing — and being attracted under the influence of Manas, Mind, the opposite pole of this spiritualized Atom, constitute a body of the same.

Karmendriyas, the five organs of action. The neutralizing attributes of the five electricities are Karmendriyas, the organs of action — excretion, generation, motion (feet), manual skill (hands), and speech. These organs, being the manifestation of the neutralizing energy of the spiritualized Atom, Chitta (the Heart), constitute an energetic body, called the body of energy, the life force or Prana.

Vishaya or Tanmatras , the five objects of the senses. The negative attributes of the five electricities are the five Tanmatras or objects of the senses of smell, taste, sight, touch, and sound, which, being united with the organs of sense through the neutralizing power of the organs of action, satisfy the desires of the heart.

Lingasarira, the fine material body. These fifteen attributes with two poles — Mind and Intelligence — of the spiritualized Atom constitute Lingasarira or Sukshmasarira, the fine material body of Purusha, the Son of God.

> SUTRAS 11, 12: "The aforementioned five objects, which are the negative attributes of the five electricities, being combined produce the idea of gross matter in its five forms: Kshiti, solids; Ap, liquids; Tejas, fire; Marut, gaseous substances; and Akasa, ether.
> These five forms of gross matter and the aforesaid fifteen attributes, together with Manas, Mind, sense consciousness; Buddhi, discriminative Intelligence; Chitta, the Heart or power of feeling; and Ahamkara, the Ego, constitute the twenty-four basic principles of creation."

Gross material body. The aforesaid five objects, which are the negative attributes of the five electricities, being combined together produce the idea of gross matter which appears to us in five different varieties: Kshiti, the solid; Ap, the liquid; Tejas, the fiery; Marat, the gaseous; and Vyoina or Akasa, the ethereal. These constitute the outer covering called Sthulasarira, the gross material body of Purusha, the Son of God.

Twenty -four Elders. These five gross matters and the aforesaid fifteen attributes together with Manas, the Mind; Buddhi, the Intelligence; Chitta, the Heart; and Ahamkara, the Ego, constitute the twenty- four principles or Elders, as mentioned in the Bible. See Revelation 4:4.

"And round about the throne were four and twenty seats; and upon the seats I saw four and twenty elders. "

The aforesaid twenty-four principles, which completed the creation of Darkness, Maya, are nothing more than the development of Ignorance, Avidya; and as this Ignorance is composed only of ideas as mentioned above, creation has in reality no substantial existence, but is a mere play of ideas on the Eternal Substance, God the Father.

> SUTRA 13: "This universe is differentiated into fourteen spheres, seven Swargas and seven Patalas."

Seven Spheres or Swargas. This universe thus described, commencing from the Eternal Substance, God, down to the gross material creation, has been distinguished into seven different spheres, Swargas or Lokas.

7th Sphere, Satyaloka. The foremost of these is Satyaloka, the sphere of God — the only ideal Substance, Sat, in the universe. No name can describe it, nor can anything in the creation of Darkness or Light

23

designate it. This sphere is therefore called Anama, the Nameless.

6th Sphere, Tapoloka. The next in order is Tapoloka, the sphere of the Holy Spirit which is the Eternal Patience, as it remains forever undisturbed by any limited idea. Because it is not approachable even by the Sons of God as such, it is called Agama, the Inaccessible.

5th Sphere, Janaloka. Next is Janaloka, the sphere of spiritual reflection, the Sons of God, wherein the idea of separate existence of Self originates. As this sphere is above the comprehension of anyone in the creation of Darkness, Maya, it is called Alakshya, the Incomprehensible.

4th Sphere, Maharloka. Then comes Maharloka, the sphere of the Atom, the beginning of the creation of Darkness, Maya, upon which the Spirit is reflected. This, the connecting link, is the only way between the spiritual and the material creation and is called the Door, Dasamadwara.

3rd Sphere, Szuarloka, Around this Atom is Swarloka, the sphere of magnetic aura, the electricities. This sphere, being characterized by the absence of all the creation (even the organs and their objects, the fine material things), is called Mahasunya, the Great Vacuum.

2nd Sphere, Bhuvarloka. The next is Bhuvarloha, the sphere of electric attributes. As the gross matters of the creation are entirely absent from this sphere, and it is conspicuous by the presence of the fine matters only, it is called Sunya, the Vacuum Ordinary.

1st Sphere, Bhuloka. The last and lowest sphere is Bhuloka, the sphere of gross material creation, which is always visible to everyone.

Sapta Patalas, seven churches. As God created man in His own image, so is the body of man like unto the image of this universe. The material body of man has also seven vital places within it called Patalas. Man, turning toward his Self and advancing in the right way, perceives the Spiritual Light in these places, which are described in the Bible as so many churches; the lights like star perceived therein are as so many angels. See 1:12,13,16,20.

"And being turned, I saw seven golden candle sticks, and in the midst of the seven candlesticks one like unto the son of man."
"And he had in his right hand seven stars..."
"The seven stars are the angels of the seven churches; and the seven candlesticks which thou sawest are the seven churches. "

Fourteen Bhuvanas, the stages of creation. The abovementioned seven spheres or Swargas and the seven Patalas constitute the fourteen Bhuvanas, the fourteen distinguishable stages of the creation.

> SUTRA 14: "Purusha is covered by five koshas or sheaths."

Five Koshas or Sheaths. This Purusha, the Son of God is screened by five coverings called the koshas or sheaths.

Heart, the 1st Kosha. The first of these five is Heart, Chitta, the Atom, composed of four ideas as mentioned before, which feels or enjoys, and thus being the seat of bliss, ananda, is called Anondamaya Kosha.

Buddhi, the 2nd Kosha. The second is the magnetic-aura electricities, manifestations of Buddhi, the Intelligence that determines what is truth. Thus, being the seat of knowledge, jnana, it is called Jnanamaya Kosha.

Manas, the 3rd Kosha. The third is the body of Manas, the Mind, composed of the organs of senses, as mentioned above, and called the Manomaya Kosha.

Prana, the 4th Kosha. The fourth is the body of energy, life force or Prana, composed of the organs of action as described before, and thus called Pranamaya Kosha.

Gross matter, the 5th Kosha. The fifth and 1 last of these sheaths is the gross matter, the Atom's outer coating, which, becoming Anna, nourishment, supports this visible world and thus is called the Annamaya Kosha.

Action of Love. The action of Repulsion, the manifestation of the Omnipotent Energy, being thus completed, the action of Attraction (the Omnipotent Love in the core of the heart) begins to be manifested. Under the influence of this Omniscient Love, the Attraction, the Atoms, being attracted toward one another, come nearer and nearer, taking ethereal, gaseous, fiery, liquid, and solid forms.

Inanimate kingdom. Thus this visible world becomes adorned with suns, planets, and moons, which we call the "inanimate" kingdom of the creation.

Vegetable kingdom. In this manner, when the action of Divine Love becomes well developed, the evolution of Avidy a, Ignorance (the particle of Darkness, Maya, the Omnipotent Energy manifested), begins to be withdrawn. Annamaya Kosha, the Atom's outer coating of gross matter being thus withdrawn, Pranamaya Kosha (the sheath composed of Karmendriyas, the organs of action) begins to operate. In this organic state the Atoms, embracing each other more closely to their heart, appear as the vegetable kingdom in the creation.

Animal kingdom. When the Pranamaya Kosha becomes withdrawn, the Manomaya Kosha (the sheath composed of Jnanendriyas , the organs of sense) comes to light. The Atoms then perceive the nature of the external world and, attracting other Atoms of different nature, form bodies as necessary for enjoyment, and thus the animal kingdom appears in the creation.

Mankind. When Manomaya Kosha becomes withdrawn, Jnanamaya Kosha (the body of Intelligence composed of electricities) becomes perceptible. The Atom, acquiring the power of determining right and wrong, becomes man, the rational being in the creation.

Devata or Angel. When man, cultivating the Divine Spirit or Omniscient Love within his heart, is able to withdraw this Jnanamaya Kosha, then the innermost sheath, Chitta, the Heart (composed of four ideas), becomes manifest. Man is then called Devata or Angel in the creation.

Free, Sannyasi. When the Heart or innermost sheath is also withdrawn, there is no longer anything to keep man in bondage to this creation of Darkness, Maya. He then becomes free, Sannyasi, the Son of God, and enters into the creation of Light.

> SUTRAS 15, 16: "Just as the objects seen in our dreams are found, when we awake, to be insubstantial, so our waking perceptions are likewise unreal — a matter of inference only."

Sleeping and waking states. When man compares his ideas relating to gross matters conceived in the wakeful state with his conception of ideas in dream, the similarity existing between them naturally leads him to conclude that this external world also is not what it appears to be.

When he looks for further explanation, he finds that all his wakeful conceptions are substantially nothing but mere ideas caused by the union of five objects of sense (the negative attributes of the five internal electricities) with the five organs of sense (their positive attributes) through the medium of five organs of action (the neutralizing attributes of the electricities).

This union is effected by the operation of Mind (Manas) and conceived or grasped by the Intelligence (Buddhi). Thus it is clear that all conceptions which man forms in his wakeful state are mere inferential Parokshajnana — a matter of inference only.

> SUTRA 17: "What is needed is a Guru, a Savior, who will awaken us to Bhakti (devotion) and to perceptions of Truth."

When man finds his Sat-Guru or Savior. When man understands by his Aparokshajnana (true comprehension) the nothingness of the external world, he appreciates the position of John the Baptist, the divine personage who witnessed Light and bore testimony of Christ, after his heart's love, the heavenly gift of Nature, had become developed.

Any advanced sincere seeker may be fortunate in having the Godlike company of some one of such personages, who may kindly stand to him as his

Spiritual Preceptor, Sat-Guru, the Savior. Following affectionately the holy precepts of these divine personages, man becomes able to direct all his organs of sense inward to their common center — the sensorium, Trikuti or Sushumnadwara, the door of the interior world — where he comprehends the Voice, like a peculiar "knocking" sound, [the Cosmic Vibration that is] the Word, Amen, Om; and sees the God-sent luminous body of Radha, symbolized in the Bible as the Forerunner or John the Baptist. See Revelation 3:14,20 and John 1:6,8,23.

"These things saith the Amen, the faithful and true - witness, the beginning of the creation of God. . . . Behold, I stand at the door, and knock; if any man hear my voice and open the door, I will come in to him and will sup with him, and he with me."

"There was a man sent from God, whose name was John... He was not that Light, but was sent to bear witness of that Light... He said, I am the voice of one crying in the wilderness, Make straight the way of the Lord. "

Ganga, Jamuna, or Jordan, the holy streams. From the peculiar nature of this sound, issuing as it does like a stream from a higher unknown region and losing itself in the gross material creation, it is figuratively designated by various sects of people by the names of different rivers that they consider as sacred; for example, Ganga by the Hindus, Jamuna by the Vaishnavas, and Jordan by the Christians.

The 2nd birth. Through his luminous body, man, believing in the existence of the true Light — the Life of this universe — becomes baptized or absorbed in the holy stream of the sound. The baptism is, so to speak, the second birth of man and is called Bhakti Yoga, without which man can never comprehend the real internal world, the kingdom of God. See John 1:9 and 3:3.

"That was the true Light, which lighteth every man that cometh into the world. "

"Verily, verily, I say unto thee, Except a man be born again, he cannot see the kingdom of God. "

Aparokshajnana, the real comprehension. In this state the son of man begins to repent and, turning back from the gross material creation, creeps toward his Divinity, the Eternal Substance, God. When the developments of ignorance are stopped, man gradually comprehends the true character of this creation of Darkness, Maya, as a mere play of ideas of the Supreme Nature on His own Self, the only Real Substance. This true comprehension is called Aparokshajnana.

> SUTRA 18: "Emancipation (Kaivalya) is obtained when one realizes the oneness of his Self with the Universal Self, the Supreme Reality."

Sannyasi or Christ the anointed Savior. When all the developments of Ignorance are withdrawn, the heart, being perfectly clear and purified, no longer merely reflects the Spiritual Light but actively manifests the same, and thus being consecrated and anointed, man becomes Sannyasi, free, or Christ the Savior. See John 1:33.

"Upon whom thou shalt see the Spirit descending, and remaining on him, the same is he which baptizeth with the Holy Ghost. "

Baptized in the stream of Light. Through this Savior the son of man becomes again baptized or absorbed in the stream of Spiritual Light, and, rising above the creation of Darkness, Maya, enters into the spiritual world and becomes unified with Abhasa Chaitanya or Purusha, the Son of God, as was the case with Lord Jesus of Nazareth. In this state man is saved for ever and ever from the bondage of Darkness, Maya. See John 1:12 and 3:5.

"But as many as received him to them gave he power to become the Sons of God, even to them that believe on his name."

"Verily, verily, I say unto thee, except a man be born of water and of the Spirit, he cannot enter into the kingdom of God. "

Sacrifice of self. When man thus entering into the spiritual world becomes a Son of God, he comprehends the universal Light — the Holy Ghost — as a perfect whole, and his Self as nothing but a mere idea resting on a fragment of the Om Light. Then he sacrifices himself to the Holy Ghost, the altar of God; that is, abandons the vain idea of his separate existence, and becomes one integral whole.

Kaivalya, the unification. Thus, being one with the universal Holy Spirit of God the Father, he becomes unified with the Real Substance, God. This unification of Self with the Eternal Substance, God, is called Kaiualya. See Revelation 3:21.

"To him that overcometh -will I grant to sit with me in my throne, even as I also overcame, and am set down with my Father in his throne."

CHAPTER 2
THE GOAL

SUTRA 1: "Hence there is desire for emancipation."

Liberation, the prime object. When man understands even by way of inference the true nature of this creation, the true relation existing between this creation and himself; and when he further understands that he is completely blinded by the influence of Darkness, Maya, and that it is the bondage of Darkness alone which makes him forget his real Self and brings about all his sufferings, he naturally wishes to be relieved from all these evils. This relief from evil, or liberation from the bondage of Maya, becomes the prime object of his life.

SUTRA 2: "Liberation is stabilization of Purusha (jiva, soul) in its real Self."

Residing in Self is liberation. When man raises himself above the idea creation of this Darkness, Maya, and passes completely out of its influence, he becomes liberated from bondage and is placed in his real Self, the Eternal Spirit.

SUTRA 3: "Then there is cessation of all pain and the attainment of the ultimate aim (true fulfillment, God-realization)."

Liberation is salvation. On attaining this liberation, man becomes saved from all his troubles, and all the desires of his heart are fulfilled, so the ultimate aim of his life is accomplished.

SUTRA 4: "Otherwise, birth after birth, man experiences the misery of unfulfilled desires."

Why man suffers. So long, however, as man identifies himself with his material body and fails to find repose in his true Self, he feels his wants according as his heart's desires remain unsatisfied. To satisfy them he has to appear often in flesh and blood on the stage of life, subject to the influence of Darkness, Maya, and has to suffer all the troubles of life and death not only in the present but in the future as well.

SUTRAS 5, 6: "Troubles are born from Avidya, Ignorance. Ignorance is the perception of the nonexistent, and the nonperception of the Existent."

What is ignorance? Ignorance, Avidya, is misconception, or is the erroneous conception of the existence of that which does not exist. Through Avidya man believes that this material creation is the only thing that substantially exists, there being nothing beyond, forgetting that this material creation is substantially nothing and is a mere play of ideas on the Eternal Spirit, the only Real Substance, beyond the comprehension of the material creation. This Ignorance is not only a trouble in itself but is also the source of all the other troubles of man.

SUTRAS 7-12: "Avidya, Ignorance, having the twofold power of polarity, manifests as egoism, attachment, aversion, and (blind) tenacity.

The darkening power of Maya produces egoism and (blind) tenacity; the polarity power of Maya produces attachment (attraction) and aversion (repulsion).

Egoism results from a lack of discrimination between the physical body and the real Self.

Tenacity is a result of natural conditioning (belief in Nature and her laws as final, instead of belief in the all-causative powers of the Soul).

Attachment means thirst for the objects of happiness.

Aversion means desire for the removal of the objects of unhappiness."

Ignorance is the source of all troubles. In order to understand how this Ignorance is the source of all other troubles we should remember (as has been explained in the previous chapter) that Ignorance, Avidya, is nothing but a particle of Darkness, Maya, taken distributiveiy, and as such it possesses the two properties of Maya. The one is its darkening power, by the influence of which man is prevented from grasping anything beyond the material creation. This darkening power produces Asmita or Egoism, the identification of Self with the material body, which is but the development of Atom, the particles of the universal force; and Abhinivesa or blind tenacity to the belief in the validity and ultimate worth of the material creation.

By virtue of the second of the properties of Maya, Ignorance or Avidya in its polarized state produces attraction for certain objects and repulsion for others. The objects so attracted are the objects of pleasure, for which an Attachment, Raja, is formed. The objects that are repulsed are the objects producing pain, for which an Aversion, Dwesha, is formed.

SUTRA 13: "The root of pain is egoistic actions, which (being based on delusions) lead to misery."

Why man is bound. By the influence of these five troubles — Ignorance, Egoism, Attachment, Aversion, and Tenacity to the material creation — man is induced to involve himself in egoistic works and in consequence he suffers.

SUTRAS 14, 15: "Man's purpose is complete freedom from unhappiness. Once he has banished all pain beyond possibility of return, he has attained the highest goal."

Ultimate aim of the heart. With man the cessation of all suffering is Artha, the heart's immediate aim. The complete extirpation of all these sufferings so that their recurrence becomes impossible, is Paramartha, the ultimate goal.

SUTRAS 16-21: "Existence, consciousness, and bliss are the three longings (of the human heart).

Ananda, bliss, is the contentment of heart attained by the ways and means suggested by the Savior, the Sat-Guru.

Chit, true consciousness, brings about the complete destruction of all troubles and the rise of all virtues.

Sat, existence, is attained by realization of the permanency of the soul.

These three qualities constitute the real nature of man.

All desires being fulfilled, and all miseries removed, the achievement of Paramartha (the highest goal) is made."

The real necessities. Man naturally feels great necessity for Sat, Existence; Chit, Consciousness; and Ananda, Bliss. These three are the real necessities of the human heart and have nothing to do with anything outside his Self. They are essential properties of his own nature, as explained in the previous chapter.

How man attains Bliss. When man becomes fortunate in securing the favor of any divine personage, Sat-Guru (the Savior), and affectionately following his holy precepts is able to direct all his attention inward, he becomes capable of satisfying all the wants of his heart and can thereby gain contentment, Ananda, the Real Bliss.

How Consciousness appears. With his heart thus contented, man becomes able to fix his attention upon anything he chooses and can comprehend all its aspects. So Chit, Consciousness of all the modifications of Nature up to its first and primal manifestation, the Word (Amen, Om), and even of his own Real Self, gradually appears. And being absorbed in the stream thereof, man becomes baptized and begins to repent and return toward his Divinity, the Eternal Father, whence he had fallen. See Revelation 2:5.

"Remember therefore from whence thou art fallen, and repent."

How Existence is realized. Man, being conscious of his own real position and of the nature of this creation of Darkness, Maya, becomes possessed of absolute power over it, and gradually withdraws all the developments of Ignorance. In this way, freed from the control of this creation of Darkness, he comprehends his own Self as Indestructible and Ever-Existing Real Substance. So Sat, the Existence of Self, comes to light.

How main object of the heart is attained. All the necessities of the heart — Sat, Existence; Chit, Consciousness; and Ananda, Bliss — having been attained, Ignorance, the mother of evils, becomes emaciated and consequently all troubles of this material world, which are the sources of all sorts of sufferings, cease forever. Thus the ultimate aim of the heart is effected.

> SUTRA 22: "All fulfillments of his nature attained, man is not merely a reflector of divine light but becomes actively united with Spirit. This state is Kaivalya, oneness."

How man finds salvation. In this state, all the necessities having been attained and the ultimate aim effected, the heart becomes perfectly purified and, instead of merely reflecting the spiritual light, actively manifests the same. Man, being thus consecrated or anointed by the Holy Spirit, becomes Christ, the anointed Savior. Entering the kingdom of Spiritual Light, he becomes the Son of God.

In this state man comprehends his Self as a fragment of the Universal Holy Spirit, and, abandoning the vain idea of his separate existence, unifies himself with the Eternal Spirit; that is, becomes one and the same with God the Father. This unification of Self with God is Kaivalya, which is the Ultimate Object of all created beings. See John 14:11.

"Believe me that I am in the Father, and the Father in me."

CHAPTER 3
THE PROCEDURE

SUTRAS 1-4: "Yajna, sacrifice, means penance (Tapas), deep study (Sutadhyaya), and the practice of meditation on Om (Brahmanidhana).

Penance is patience or evenmindedness in all conditions (equanimity amidst the essential dualities of Maya; cold and heat, pain and pleasure, etc.).

Szvadhyaya consists of reading or hearing spiritual truth, pondering it, and forming a definite conception of it.

(Meditation on) Pranava, the divine sound of Om, is the only way to Brahman (Spirit), salvation."

Patience, faith, and holy work explained. Tapas is religious mortification or patience both in enjoyments and in sufferings. Swadhyaya is sravana, study, with manana, deep attention, and thereby nididhyasana, forming of an idea of the true faith about Self; that is, what I am, whence I came, where I shall go, what I have come for, and other such matters concerning Self. Brahmanidhana is the baptism or merging of Self in the stream of the Holy Sound (Pranava, Aurn), which is the holy work performed to attain salvation and the only way by which man can return to his Divinity, the Eternal Father, whence he has fallen. See Revelation 2:19.

"I know thy works, and charity, and service, and faith, and thy patience, and thy works; and the last to be more than the first."

SUTRAS 5, 6: "Om is heard through cultivation of Sraddha (heart's natural love), Virya (moral courage), Smriti (memory of one's divinity), and Samadhi (true concentration).

Sraddha is intensification of the heart's natural love."

How the Holy Sound manifests. This Holy Sound Pranava Sabda manifests spontaneously through culture of Sraddha, the energetic tendency of the heart's natural love; Virya, moral courage; Smriti, true conception; and Samadhi, true concentration.

The virtue of Love. The heart's natural love is the principal requisite to attain a holy life. When this love, the heavenly gift of Nature, appears in the heart, it removes all causes of excitation from the system and cools it down to a perfectly normal state; and, invigorating the vital powers, expels all foreign matters — the germs of diseases — by natural ways (perspiration and so forth). It thereby makes man perfectly healthy in body and mind, and enables him to understand properly the guidance of Nature.

When this love becomes developed in man it makes him able to understand the real position of his own Self as well as of others surrounding him.

With the help of this developed love, man becomes fortunate in gaining the Godlike company of the divine personages and is saved forever. Without this love, man cannot live in the natural way, neither can he keep company with the fit person for his own welfare; he becomes often excited by the foreign matters taken into his system through mistakes in understanding the guidance of Nature, and in consequence he suffers in body and mind. He can never find any peace whatever, and his life becomes a burden. Hence the culture of this love, the heavenly gift, is the principal requisite for the attainment of holy salvation; it is impossible for man to advance a step toward the same without it. See Revelation 2:2-4.

"I know thy works, and thy labor, and thy patience, and how thou canst not bear them which are evil: and thou hast tried them which say they are apostles, and are not, and hast found them liars.

"And hast borne and hast patience, and for my name's sake hast labored, and hast not fainted.

"Nevertheless I have somewhat against thee, because thou hast left thy first love."

> SUTRAS 7,8: "Moral courage (Virya) arises from Sraddha, directing one's love toward the guru, and from affectionately following his instructions.
>
> Those who remove our troubles, dispel our doubts, and bestow peace are true teachers. They perform a Godlike work. Their opposites (those who increase our doubts and difficulties) are harmful to us and should be avoided like poison."

As explained in the previous chapter, this creation is substantially nothing but a mere ideaplay of Nature on the only Real Substance, God, the Eternal Father, who is Guru — the Supreme idea play is universe. All things of this creation are therefore no other substance than this Guru, the Supreme Father, God Himself, perceived in plurality by the manifold aspects of the play of Nature. See John 10:34 and Psalm 82:6.

"Jesus answered them, Is it not written in your law, I said, Ye are gods?"

"I have said, Ye are gods; and all of you are children of the most High."

Out of this creation, the object that relieves us of our miseries and doubts and administers peace to us, whether animate or inanimate, and however insignificant the same may be, is entitled to our utmost respect. Even if it be regarded by others as an object of vilest contempt, it should be accepted as Sat (Savior) and its company as Godlike. That which produces opposite results, destroying our peace, throwing us into doubts, and creating our miseries, should be considered Asat, the bane of all good, and should be avoided as such. The Indian sages have a saying:

"Some consider the deities to exist in water (i.e., natural elements) while the learned consider them to exist in heaven (astral world); the unwise seek them in wood and stones (i.e., in images or symbols), but the Yogi realizes God in the sanctuary of his own Self."

To attain salvation men choose as their Savior the objects that they can comprehend according to their own stage of evolution. Thus, in general, people think that illness is a dire calamity; and as water, when properly administered, tends to remove illness, ignorant men may choose for their Divinity water itself.

Philosophers, being able to comprehend the internal electrical Light that shines within them, find their heart's love flowing energetically toward the Light that relieves them of all causes of excitation, cools down their system to a normal state, and, invigorating their vital powers, makes them perfectly healthy, both in body and in mind. They then accept this Light as their Divinity or Savior.

Ignorant people in their blind faith would accept a piece of wood or stone as their Savior or Divinity in the external creation, for which their heart's natural love will develop till by its energetic tendency it will relieve them of all exciting causes, cool their system down to a normal state, and invigorate their vital powers. The adepts, on the other hand, having full control over the whole material world, find their Divinity or Savior in Self and not outside in the external world.

Regard the Guru with deep love. To keep company with the Guru is not only to be in his physical presence (as this is sometimes impossible), but mainly means to keep him in our hearts and to be one with him in principle and to attune ourselves with him.

This thought has been expressed by Lord Bacon: "A crowd is not a company, it is a mere gallery of faces." To keep company, therefore, with the Godlike object is to associate him with Sraddha, the heart's love intensified in the sense above explained, by keeping his appearance and attributes fully in mind, and by reflecting on the same and affectionately following his instructions, lamblike. See John 1:29.

"Behold the Lamb of God, which taketh away the sin of the world."

By so doing, when man becomes able to conceive the sublime status of his divine brothers, he may be fortunate in remaining in their company and in securing help from any one of them whom he may choose as his Spiritual Preceptor, SatGuru, the Savior.

Thus, to resume, Virya or moral courage can be obtained by the culture of Sraddha, that is, by devoting one's natural love to his Preceptor, by being always in his company (in the internal sense already explained), and by following with affection his holy instructions as they are freely and spontaneously given.

> SUTRAS 9-1 1: "Moral courage is strengthened by observance of Yama (morality or self-control) and Niyama (religious rules).
>
> Yama comprises noninjury to others, truthfulness, nonstealing, continence, and noncovetousness.
>
> Niyama means purity of body and mind, contentment in all circumstances, and obedience (following the instructions of the guru)."

Firmness of moral courage can be attained by the culture of Yama, the religious forbearances: abstention from cruelty, dishonesty, covetousness, unnatural living, and unnecessary possessions; and of Niyama, the religious observances: purity in body and mind — cleaning the body externally and internally from all foreign matters which, being fermented, create different sorts of diseases in the system, and clearing the mind from all prejudices and dogmas that make one narrow — contentment in all circumstances; and obedience to the holy precepts of the divine personages.

What is natural living? To understand what natural living is, it will be necessary to distinguish it from what is unnatural. Living depends upon the selection of (1) food, (2) dwelling, and (3) company. To live naturally, the lower animals can select these for themselves by the help of their instincts and the natural sentinels placed at the sensory entrances — the organs of sight, hearing, touch, smell, and taste. With men in general, however, these organs are so much perverted by unnatural living from very infancy that little reliance can be placed on their judgments. To understand, therefore, what our natural needs are, we ought to depend upon observation, experiment, and reason.

What is natural food for man? First, to select our natural food, our observation should be directed to the formation of the organs that aid in digestion and nutrition, the _____ d digestive canal; to the natural tendency _____ ense which guide animals to their foo _____ urishment of the young.

Observat _____ rvation of the teeth we find th _____ nals the incisors are little develope _____ es are of striking length, smooth an _____ ze the prey. The molars also are pointed; thes _____ nts, however, do not meet, but fit closely side by side to separate the muscular fibers.

In the herbivorous animals the incisors are strikingly developed, the canines are stunted (though occasionally developed into weapons, as in elephants), the molars are broad-topped and furnished with enamel on the sides only.

In the frugivorous all the teeth are of nearly the same height; the canines are little projected, conical, and blunt (obviously not intended for seizing prey but for exertion of strength). The molars are broad-topped and furnished at the top with enamel folds to prevent waste caused by their side motion, but not pointed for chewing flesh.

In omnivorous animals such as bears, on the other hand, the incisors resemble those of the herbivorous, the canines are like those of the carnivorous, and the molars are both pointed and broad-topped to serve a twofold purpose.

Now if we observe the formation of the teeth in man we find that they do not resemble those of the carnivorous, neither do they resemble the teeth of the herbivorous or the omnivorous. They do resemble, exactly, those of the frugivorous animals. The reasonable inference, therefore, is that man is a frugivorous or fruit-eating animal.

Observation of the digestive canal. By observation of the digestive canal we find that the bowels of carnivorous animals are 3 to 5 times the length of their body, measuring from the mouth to the anus; and their stomach is almost spherical. The bowels of the herbivorous are 20 to 28 times the length of their body and their stomach is more extended and of compound build. But the bowels of the frugivorous animals are 10 to 12 times the length of their body; their stomach is somewhat broader than that of the carnivorous and has a continuation in the duodenum serving the purpose of a second stomach.

This is exactly the formation we find in human beings, though Anatomy says that the human bowels are 3 to 5 times the length of man's body — making a mistake by measuring the body from the crown to the soles, instead of from mouth to anus. Thus we can again draw the inference that man is, in all probability, a frugivorous animal.

Observation of organs of sense. By observation of the natural tendency of the organs of sense — the guideposts for determining what is nutritious — by which all animals are directed to their food, we find that when the carnivorous animal finds prey, he becomes so much delighted that his eyes begin to sparkle; he boldly seizes the prey and greedily laps the jetting blood. On the contrary, the herbivorous animal refuses even his natural food, leaving it untouched, if it is sprinkled with a little blood. His senses of smell and sight lead him to select grasses and other herbs for his food, which he tastes with delight. Similarly with the frugivorous animals, we find that their senses always direct them to fruits of the trees and field.

In men of all races we find that their senses of smell, sound, and sight never lead them to slaughter animals; on the contrary they cannot bear even the sight of such killings. Slaughterhouses are always recommended to be removed far from the towns; men often pass strict ordinances forbidding the uncovered transportation of flesh meats. Can flesh then be considered the natural food of man, when both his eyes and his nose are so much against it, unless deceived by flavors of spices, salt, and sugar? On the other hand, how delightful do we find the fragrance of fruits, the very sight of which often makes the mouth water! It may also be noticed that various grains and roots possess an agreeable odor and taste, though faint, even when unprepared. Thus again, we are led to infer from these observations that man was intended to be a frugivorous animal.

Observation of the nourishment of the young. By observation of the nourishment of the young we find that milk is undoubtedly the food of the newborn babe. Abundant milk is not supplied in the breasts of the mother if she does not take fruits, grains, and vegetables as her natural food.

Cause of disease. Hence from these observations the only conclusion that can reasonably be drawn is that various grains, fruits, roots, and — for beverage — milk, and pure water openly exposed to air and sun are decidedly the best natural food for man. These, being congenial to the system when taken according to the power of the digestive organs, well chewed and mixed with saliva, are always easily assimilated.

Other foods are unnatural to man and being uncongenial to the system are necessarily foreign to it; when they enter the stomach, they are not properly assimilated. Mixed with the blood, they accumulate in the excretory and other organs not properly adapted to them. When they cannot find their way out, they subside in tissue crevices by the law of gravitation; and, being fermented, produce diseases, mental and physical, and ultimately lead to premature death.

Children's development. Experiment also proves that the nonirritant diet natural to the vegetarian is, almost without exception, admirably suited to children's development, both physical and mental. Their minds, understanding, will, the principal faculties, temper, and general disposition are also properly developed.

Natural living calms passions. We find that when extraordinary means such as excessive fasting, scourging, or monastic confinement are resorted to for the purpose of suppressing the sexual passions, these means seldom produce the desired effect. Experiment shows, however, that man can easily overcome these passions, the archenemy of morality, by natural living on a nonirritant diet, above referred to; thereby men gain a calmness of mind which every psychologist knows is the most favorable to mental activity and to a clear understanding, as well as to a judicial way of thinking.

Sexual desire. Something more should be said here about the natural instinct of propagation, which is, next to the instinct of self-preservation, the strongest in the animal body. Sexual desire, like all other desires, has a normal and an abnormal or diseased state, the latter resulting only from the foreign matter accumulated by unnatural living as mentioned above. In the sexual desire everyone has a very accurate thermometer to indicate the condition of his health. This desire is forced from its normal state by the irritation of nerves that results from the pressure of foreign matter accumulated in the system, which pressure is exerted on the sexual apparatus and is at first manifested by an increased sexual desire followed by a gradual decrease of potency.

This sexual desire in its normal state makes man quite free from all disturbing lusts, and operates on the organism (awaking a wish for appeasement) only infrequently. Here again experiment shows that this desire, like all other desires, is always normal in individuals who lead a natural life as mentioned.

The root of the tree of life. The sexual organ —the junction of important nerve extremities, particularly of the sympathetic and spinal nerves (the principal nerves of the abdomen) which, through their connection with the brain, are capable of enlivening the whole system — is in a sense the root of the tree of life. Man well instructed in the proper use of sex can keep his body and mind in proper health and can live a pleasant life throughout.

The practical principles of sexual health are not taught because the public regards the subject as unclean and indecent. Thus blinded, mankind presumes to clothe Nature in a veil because she seems to them impure, forgetting that she is always clean and that everything impure and improper lies in man's ideas, and not in Nature herself. It is clear therefore that man, not knowing the truth about the dangers of misuse of the sexual power, and being compelled to wrong practices by the nervous irritation resulting from unnatural living, suffers troublesome diseases in life and ultimately becomes a victim of premature death.

Dwelling place of man. Secondly, about our dwelling place. We can easily understand, when we feel displeasure on entering a crowded room after breathing fresh air on a mountaintop or in an expanse of field or garden, that the atmosphere of the town or any crowded place is quite an unnatural dwelling place. The fresh atmosphere of the mountaintop, or of the field or garden, or of a dry place under trees covering a large plot of land and freely ventilated with fresh air is the proper dwelling place for man according to Nature.

The company we should keep. And thirdly, as to the company we should keep. Here also, if we listen to the dictates of our conscience and consult our natural liking, we will at once find that we favor those persons whose magnetism affects us harmoniously, who cool our system, internally invigorate our vitality, develop our natural love, and thus relieve us of our miseries and administer peace to us. This is to say, we should be in the company of the Sat or Savior and should avoid that of the Asat, as described before. By keeping the company of Sat (the Savior) we are enabled to enjoy perfect health, physical and mental, and our life is prolonged. If on the other hand we disobey the warning of Mother Nature, without listening to the dictates of our pure conscience, and keep the company of whatever has been designated as Asat, an opposite effect is produced and our health is impaired and our life shortened.

Necessity of natural living and purity. Thus natural living is helpful for the practice of Yama, the ascetic forbearances as explained earlier. Purity of mind and body being equally important in the practice of Niyama, the ascetic observances already explained, every attempt should be made to attain that purity.

SUTRAS 12-18: "Hence bondage disappears.

The eight bondages or snares are hatred, shame, fear, grief, condemnation, race prejudice, pride of family, and smugness.

(Removal of the eight bondages) leads to magnanimity of heart.

Thus one becomes fit to practice Asana, Pranayama, and Pratyahara; and to enjoy the householder's life (by fulfilling all one's desires and so getting rid of them).

Asana means a steady and pleasant posture of the body.

Pranayama means control over prana, life force.

Pratyahara means withdrawal of the senses from external objects."

The eight meannesses of the heart. Firmness of moral courage, when attained, removes all the obstacles in the way of salvation. These obstacles are of eight sorts — hatred, shame, fear, grief, condemnation, race prejudice, pride of pedigree, and a narrow sense of respectability — which eight are the meannesses of the human heart.

Awakening magnanimity of the heart. By the removal of these eight obstacles, Viratwam or Mahattwam (magnanimity of the heart) comes in, and this makes man fit for the practice of Asana (remaining in steady and pleasant posture), Pranayama (control over prana, involuntary nerve electricities), and Pratyahara (changing the direction of the voluntary nerve currents inward). These practices enable man to satisfy his heart by enjoying the objects of the senses as intended for Garhasthyasrama (domestic) life.

Value of Pranayama. Man can put the voluntary nerves into action whenever he likes, and can give them rest when fatigued. When all of these voluntary nerves require rest he sleeps naturally, and by this sleep the voluntary nerves, being refreshed, can work again with full vigor. Man's involuntary nerves, however, irrespective of his will, are working continuously of themselves from his birth. As he has no control over them, he cannot interfere with their action in the least. When these nerves become fatigued they also want rest and naturally fall asleep. This sleep of the involuntary nerves is called Mahanidra, the great sleep, or death. When this takes place, the circulation, respiration, and other vital functions being stopped, the material body naturally begins to decay. After a while, when this great sleep Mahanidra is over, man awakes, with all his desires, and is reborn in a new physical body for the accomplishment of his various yearnings. In this way man binds himself to life and death and fails to achieve final salvation.

Control over death. But if man can control these involuntary nerves by the aforesaid Pranayama, he can stop the natural decay of the material body and put the involuntary nerves (of the heart, lungs, and other vital organs) to rest periodically, as he does with his voluntary nerves in sleep. After such rest by Pranayama the involuntary nerves become refreshed and work with newly replenished life.

As after sleep, when rest has been taken by the voluntary nerves, man requires no help to awaken naturally; so after death also, when man has enjoyed a full rest, he awakens naturally to life in a new body on earth. If man can "die," that is, consciously put his entire nervous system, voluntary and involuntary, to rest each day by practice of Pranayama, his whole physical system works with great vigor.

Life and death come under the control of the yogi who perseveres in the practice of Pranayama, In that way he saves his body from the premature decay that overtakes most men, and can remain as long as he wishes in his present physical form, thus having time to work out his karma in one body and to fulfill (and so get rid of) all the various desires of his heart. Finally purified, he is no longer required to come again into this world under the influence of Maya, Darkness, or to suffer the "second death." See I Corinthians 15:31, and Revelation 2:10, 11.

"I protest by our rejoicing which I have in Christ [consciousness]. I die daily." — St. Paul.

"Be thou faithful unto death, and. I will give thee a crown of life.... He that overcometh shall not be hurt of the second death. "

Necessity of Pratyahara. Man enjoys a thing when he so desires. At the time of the enjoyment, however, if he directs his organs of sense, through which he enjoys, toward the object of his desire, he can never be satisfied, and his desires increase in double force. On the contrary, if he can direct his organs of sense inward toward his Self, at that time he can satisfy his heart immediately. So the practice of the aforesaid Pratyahara, the changing of the direction of the voluntary nerve currents inward, is a desirable way to fulfill his worldly desires. Man must reincarnate again and again until all his earthly longings are worked out and he is free from all desires.

Necessity of Asana. Man cannot feel or even think properly when his mind is not in a pleasant state; and the different parts of the human body are so harmoniously arranged that if even any minutest part of it be hurt a little, the whole system becomes disturbed. So to comprehend a thing, that is, to feel a thing by the heart clearly, the practice of the aforesaid Asana, the steady and pleasant posture, is necessary

> SUTRAS 19-22: "Smriti, true conception, leads to knowledge of all creation.
>
> Samadhi, true concentration, enables one to abandon individuality for universality.
>
> Hence arises Samyama ("restraint" or overcoming the egoistic self), by which one experiences the Om vibration that reveals God.
>
> Thus the soul (is baptized) in Bhakti Yoga (devotion). This is the state of Divinity."

Smriti, the true conception. Man, when expert in the above-mentioned practices, becomes able to conceive or feel all things of this creation by his heart. This true conception is called Smrili.

Samadhi, true concentration. Fixing attention firmly on any object thus conceived, when man becomes as much identified with it as if he were devoid of his individual nature, he attains the state of Samadhi or true concentration.

Pranava Sabda, the Word of God. When man directs all his organs of sense toward their common center, the sensorium or Sushumnadwara, the door of the internal world, he perceives his Godsent luminous body of Radha or John the Baptist, and hears the peculiar "knocking" sound, Prariaua Sabda, the Word of God. See John 1:6, 7, 23.

"There was a man sent from God, whose name was John,

"The same came for a -witness, to bear witness of the Light, that all men through him might believe. "

"I am the voice of one crying in the wilderness."

Samyama, the concentration of the self. Thus perceiving, man naturally believes in the existence of the true Spiritual Light, and, withdrawing his self from the outer world, concentrates himself on the sensorium. This concentration of the self is called Samyama.

Bhakti Yoga or baptism, the second birth of man. By this Samyama or concentration of self on the sensorium, man becomes baptized or absorbed in the holy stream of the Divine Sound. This baptism is called Bhakti Yoga.

In this state man repents; that is, turning from this gross material creation of Darkness, Maya, he climbs back toward his Divinity, the Eternal Father, whence he had fallen, and passing through the sensorium, the door, enters into an internal sphere, Bhuvarloka. This entrance into the internal world is the second birth of man. In this state man becomes Devata, a divine being.

> SUTRA 23: "Translation same as following commentary."

Five states of human heart. There are five states of the human heart: dark, propelled, steady, devoted, and clean. By these different states of the heart man is classified, and his evolutionary status determined.

> SUTRA 24: "In the dark state of the heart, man harbors misconceptions (about everything). This state is a result of Avidya, Ignorance, and produces a Sudra (a man of the lowest caste). He can grasp only ideas of the physical world. This state of mind is prevalent in Kali Yuga, the Dark Age of a cycle."

The dark heart. In the dark state of the heart man misconceives; he thinks that this gross material portion of the creation is the only real substance in existence, and that there is nothing besides. However, this is contrary to the truth, as has been explained before, and is nothing but the effect of Ignorance, Avidya.

Sudra or servant class. In this state man is called Sudra, or belonging to the servant class, because his natural duty then is to serve the higher class people in order to secure their company and thereby prepare his heart to attain a higher stage.

Kali Yuga, the dark cycle. This state of in an is called Kali; and whenever in any solar system man generally remains in this state and is ordinarily deprived of the power of advancing beyond the same, the whole of that system is said to be in Kali Yuga, the dark cycle.

> SUTRAS 25, 26: "Passing beyond the first stage in Brahma's plan, man strives for enlightenment and enters the natural Kshatriya (warrior) caste.
>
> He is propelled (by evolutionary forces) to struggle (for truth). He seeks a guru and appreciates his divine counsel. Thus a Kshatriya becomes fit to dwell in the worlds of higher understanding."

The propelled heart. When man becomes a little enlightened he compares his experiences relating to the material creation, gathered in his wakeful state, with his experiences in dream, and understanding the latter to be merely ideas, begins to entertain doubts as to the substantial existence of the former. His heart then becomes propelled to learn the real nature of the universe and, struggling to clear his doubts, seeks for evidence to determine what is truth.

Kshatriya, the military class. In this state man is called Kshatriya, or one of the military class; and to struggle in the manner aforesaid becomes his natural duty, by whose performance he may get an insight into the nature of creation and attain the real knowledge of it.

Sandhisthala— the place between higher and lower. This Kshatriya state of man is called Sandhisthala, the place between higher and lower. In this state men, becoming anxious for real knowledge, need help of one another; hence mutual love, the principal necessity for gaining salvation, appears in the heart.

Motivated by the energetic tendency of this love, man affectionately keeps company with those who destroy troubles, clear doubts, and afford peace to him, and hence avoids whatever produces the contrary result; he also studies scientifically the scriptures of divine personages.

When man finds Sat-Guru, the Savior. In this way man becomes able to appreciate what true faith is, and understands the real position of the divine personages when he is fortunate in securing the Godlike company of some one of them who will kindly stand to him as his Spiritual Preceptor, Sat-Guru, or Savior. Following affectionately the holy precepts, he learns to concentrate his mind, directing his organs of sense to their common center or sensorium, Sushumnadwara, the door of the internal sphere. There he perceives the luminous body of John the Baptist, or Radha, and hears the holy Sound (Amen, Om) like a stream or river; and being absorbed or baptized in it, begins to move back toward his Divinity, the Eternal Father, through the different Lokas or spheres of the creation.

> SUTRA 27: "The worlds or Lokas of creation are seven: Bhu, Bhuvar, Swar, Mahar y Jana y Tapo y and Satya. (This earth, and the "earthy" stage of man's consciousness, are called Bhuloka.)"

The Seven Lokas. In the way toward Divinity there are seven spheres or stages of creation, designated as Stuargas or Lokas by the Oriental sages, as described in Chapter 1:13. These are Bhuloka, the sphere of gross matters; Bhuvarloka, the sphere of fine matters or electric attributes ; Swarloka, the sphere of magnetic poles and auras or electricities; Maharloka, the sphere of magnets, the atoms; Janaloka, the sphere of Spiritual Reflections, the Sons of God; Tapoloka, the sphere of the Holy Ghost, the Universal Spirit; and Satyaloka, the sphere of God, the Eternal Substance, Sat. Of these seven planes, the first three (Bhuloka, Bhuvarloka, and Swarloka) comprise the material creation, the kingdom of Darkness, Maya; and the last three (Janaloka, Tapoloka, and Satyaloka) comprise the spiritual creation, the kingdom of Light. Maharloka or the sphere of Atom, being in the midst, is said to be the Moor" communicating between these two — the material and spiritual creation — and is called Dasamadwara, the tenth door, or Brahmarandhra, the way to Divinity.

> SUTRA 28: ""Entering Bhuvarloka ("air" or "the world of becoming") man becomes a Dwija or "twice born." He comprehends the second portion of material creation — that of finer, subtler forces. This state of mind is prevalent in Dwapara Yuga."

Dwija or twice-born. When man, being baptized, begins to repent and move back toward the Eternal Father and, withdrawing his self from the gross material world, Bhuloha, enters into the world of fine matter, Bhuvarloka, he is said to belong to the Dwija or twice-born class. In this state he comprehends his internal electricities, the second fine material portion of the creation; and understands that the existence of the external is substantially nothing but mere coalescence or union of his fine internal objects of sense (the negative attributes of electricities) with his five organs of sense (the positive attributes) through his five organs of action (the neutralizing attributes of the same), caused by the operation of his mind and conscience (consciousness).

The steady heart. This state of man is Dwapara; and when this becomes the general state of human beings naturally in any solar system, the whole of that system is said to be in Dwapara Yuga. In this Diuapara state the heart becomes steady.

If man continues in the baptized state, remaining immersed in the holy stream, he gradually comes to a pleasant state wherein his heart wholly abandons the ideas of the external world and becomes devoted to the internal one.

> SUTRA 29: "In Swarloka ("heaven") man is fit to understand the mysteries of Chitta, the magnetic third portion of material creation. He becomes a Vipra (nearly perfect being). This state of mind is prevalent in Treta Yuga."

The devoted heart. In this devoted state man, withdrawing his self from Bhuvarloka, the world of electric attributes, comes to Swarloka, the world of magnetic attributes, the electricities and poles; he then becomes able to comprehend Chitta, Heart, the magnetic third portion of creation. This Chitta, as explained in Chapter 1 , is the spiritualized Atom, Avidya or Ignorance, a part of Darkness, Maya. Man, comprehending this Chitta, becomes able to understand the whole of Darkness, Maya itself, of which Chitta is a part, as well as the entire creation. Man is then said to belong to the Vipra, or nearly perfect, class. This state of human beings is called Treta; when this becomes the general state of human beings naturally in any solar system, the whole of that system is said to be in Treta Yuga.

SUTRA 30: "Through true repentance man reaches Maharloka (the "great world"). No longer subject to the influence of ignorance, Maya, he attains a clean heart. He enters the natural caste of the Brahmanas ("knowers of Brahma"). This state of mind is prevalent in Satya Yuga."

The Clean Heart. Man continuing Godward further lifts up his self to Maharloka, the region of magnet, the Atom; then all the developments of Ignorance being withdrawn, his heart comes to a clean state, void of all external ideas. Then man becomes able to comprehend the Spiritual Light, Brahma, the Real Substance in the universe, which is the last and everlasting spiritual portion in creation. In this stage man is called Brahmana or of the spiritual class. This stage of the human being is called Satya, and when this becomes the general state of man naturally in any solar system, the whole of that system is said to be in Satya Yuga.

SUTRAS 31, 32: "Not merely reflecting but manifesting Spiritual Light, man rises to Janaloka, the kingdom of God. Then he passes into Tapoloka, the sphere of Kutastha Chaitanya. Abandoning the vain idea of his separate existence, he enters Satyaloka, wherein he attains the state of final release or Kaivalya, oneness with Spirit."

In this way, when the heart becomes purified, it no longer merely reflects but manifests Spiritual Light, the Son of God; and thus being consecrated or anointed by the Spirit it becomes Christ, the Savior. This is the only way through which man, being again baptized or absorbed in Spirit, can rise above the creation of Darkness and enter into Janaloka, the Kingdom of God;

that is, the creation of Light. In this state man is called Jivanmukta Sannyasi, like Lord Jesus of Nazareth. See John 3:5 and 14:6.

"Verily, verily, I say unto thee, Except a man be born of water and of the Spirit, he cannot enter into the kingdom of God."

"Jesus saith unto him, I am the way, the truth, and the life: no man cometh unto the Father, but by me."

In this state man comprehends himself as nothing but a mere ephemeral idea resting on a fragment of the universal Holy Spirit of God, the Eternal Father, and understanding the real worship, he sacrifices his self there at this Holy Spirit, the altar of God; that is, abandoning the vain idea of his separate existence, he becomes "dead" or dissolved in the universal Holy Spirit; and thus reaches Tapoloka, the region of the Holy Ghost.

In this manner, being one and the same with the universal Holy Spirit of God, man becomes unified with the Eternal Father Himself, and so comes to Satyaloka, in which he comprehends that all this creation is substantially nothing but a mere idea-play of his own nature, and that nothing in the universe exists besides his own Self. This state of unification is called Kaiualya, the Sole Self. See Revelation 14:13 and John 16:28.

"Blessed are the dead which die in the Lord from henceforth. "

"I came forth from, the Father; and am come into the world: again, I leave the world, and go to the Father. "

CHAPTER 4
THE REVELATION

> SUTRAS 1-3: "Adeptship is achieved by purification of man's three bodies. It is also attainable through the grace of the guru.
> Purification comes through Nature, penance, and mantras.
> Through Nature there is purification of dense matter (the physical body); through penance, purification of the fine matter (the subtle body); through mantras, purification of the mind."

Adeptship is attainable by the purification of the body in all respects. Purification of the material body can be effected by things generated along with it by Nature; that of the electric body by patience in all circumstances; and that of the magnetic body (chitta, spiritualized Atom, Heart) by regulation of the breath, which is called mantra, the purifier of the mind. The process of how these purifications can be effected may be learnt at the feet of the divine personages who witness Light and bear testimony of the Christ Consciousness.

> SUTRAS 4, 5: "Through the holy effect of the mantra, the Pranava or Aum sound becomes audible. The sacred sound is heard in various ways, according to the devotee's stage of advancement (in purifying his heart)."

By culture of regulation of the breath as directed by the Spiritual Preceptor (Sat-Guru), the holy Word (Pranava or Sabda) spontaneously appears and becomes audible. When this mantra (Word, Pranava) appears, the breath becomes regulated and checks the decay of the material body.

This Pranava appears in different forms at the different stages of advancement, according to the purification of the heart (Chitta).

> SUTRA 6: "One who cultivates the heart's natural love obtains the guidance of a guru, and starts his sadhana (path of spiritual discipline). He becomes a Pravartaka, an initiate."

It has already been explained what Sat-Guru is and how to keep the company thereof. Man, when endowed with the heavenly gift of pure love, naturally becomes disposed to avoid the company of what is Asat and to keep the company of what has been described as Sat. By affectionately keeping the company of Sat he may be fortunate enough to please one who may kindly stand to him as his Sat-Guru or Spiritual Preceptor. By keeping his preceptor's Godlike company there grows an inclination, Pravritti, in the disciple's heart to save himself from the creation of darkness, Maya, and he becomes Pravartaka, an initiate in the practices of Yama and Niyama, the ascetic forbearances and observances necessary to obtain salvation.

> SUTRA 7: "By the practice of Yama and Niyama, the eight meannesses of the human heart disappear and virtue arises. Man thus becomes a Sadhaka, a true disciple, fit to attain salvation."

It may be remembered that by the culture of Varna and Niyama, the eight meannesses vanish from the human heart and magnanimity comes in. It is at this stage that man becomes fit for the practice of ascetic posture and the other processes pointed out by his Sat-Guru to attain salvation; when he continues to practice the processes so pointed out to him by his Sat-Guru he becomes a Sadhaka or disciple.

> SUTRA 8: "He progresses in godliness, hears the holy Om sound, and becomes a Siddha, divine personage."

On reference to Chapter 3 it will be found how a disciple, while passing through the different stages, becomes able to conceive the different objects of creation in his heart; and how he gradually advances through the states of meditation; and how, ultimately, by concentrating his attention on the sensorium, he perceives the peculiar sound, Pranava or Sabda, the holy Word, at which time the heart becomes divine and the Ego, Ahamkara, or son of man becomes merged or baptized in the stream thereof, and the disciple becomes Siddha, an adept, a divine personage.

> SUTRA 9: "Then he perceives the manifestations of Spirit, and passes through the seven Patala Lokas (or centers in the spine), beholding the seven rishis."

In the state of baptism (Bhakti Yoga, or Sural Sabda Yoga, absorption of the Ego in the holy Sound) man repents and withdraws his self from the external world of gross matters, Bhuloka, and enters into the internal one of fine matter, the Bhuvarloka. There he perceives the manifestation of Spirit, the true Light, like seven stars in seven centers or astrally shining places, which are compared to seven golden candlesticks. These stars, being the manifestation of true Light, the Spirit, are called angels or rishis, which appear one after another in the right hand of the son of man; that is, in his right way to Divinity,

The seven golden candlesticks are the seven shining places in the body, known as brain, the sahasrara; medulla oblongata, the ajna chakra; and five spinal centers — cervical, visuddha; dorsal, anahata; lumbar, manipura; sacral, swadhishthana; and coccygeal, muladhara, where the Spirit becomes manifested. Through these seven centers or churches, the Ego or son of man passes toward the Divinity. See Revelation 1:12, 13, 16, 20, and 2:1.

"And being turned, I saw seven golden candlesticks; and in the midst of the seven candlesticks one like unto the son of man And he had in his right hand seven stars."

"The mystery of the seven stars which thou sawest in my right hand, and the seven golden candlesticks. The seven stars are the angels of the seven churches; and the seven candlesticks which thou sawest are the seven churches."

"These things saith he that holdeth the seven stars in his right hand, who walketh in the midst of the seven golden candlesticks."

In this state of baptism (Bhakti Yoga or Surat Sabda Yoga) the Ego, Surat, the son of man, gradually passing through the seven places mentioned, acquires the knowledge thereof; and when he thus completes the journey through the whole of these regions he understands the true nature of the universe. Withdrawing his self from Bhuvarloka, the fine material creation, he enters into Swarloka, the source of all matters, fine and gross. There he perceives the luminous astral form around his Heart, Atom, the throne of Spirit the Creator, provided with five electricities and with two poles, Mind and Intelligence, of seven different colors as in rainbows. In this sphere of electricities, mind, and intelligence, the source of all objects of senses and of organs for their enjoyment, man becomes perfectly satisfied with being in possession of all objects of his desires, and acquires a complete knowledge thereof. Hence the aforesaid astral form with its electricities and poles, the seven parts thereof, has been described as a sealed casket of knowledge, a book with seven seals. See Revelation 4:3 and 5:1.

"And there was a rainbow round about the throne. "

"And I saw in the right hand of him that sat on the throne a book written within and on the back side, sealed with seven seals."

> SUTRA 10: "Then, because of yoga knowledge and power, man obtains supremacy over the seven Swargas (heavens). He achieves salvation by dissolving the four original ideas (the "four manus" or primal thoughts by which creation sprang into being)."

Passing through this Swarloka, the son of man comes to Maharloka, the place of magnet (the Atom), of which the ideas of manifestation (Word), Time, Space, and particle (Atom) are the four component parts. As mentioned in Chapter 1, this Maharloka represents Avidya, Ignorance, which produces the idea of separate existence of self and is the source of Ego, the son of man. Thus man (manava), being the offspring of Ignorance, and Ignorance being represented by the four ideas aforesaid, these ideas are called the four manus the origins or sources of man.

SUTRA 11: "Being thus victorious over the powers of Darkness and Ignorance, man becomes one with God."

Maharloka, the place of Magnet (Atom), is the Brahynarandhra or Dasamadwara, the door between two creations, material and spiritual. When Ego, the son of man, comes to the door, he comprehends the Spiritual Light and becomes baptized therein. And passing through this door he comes above the ideational creation of Darkness, Maya, and entering into the spiritual world, receives the true Light and becomes the Son of God. Thus man, being the Son of God, overcomes all bondage of Darkness, Maya, and becomes possessed of all aiswaryas, the ascetic majesties. These aiswaryas are of eight sorts:

Anima, the power of making one's body or anything else as small as he likes, even as tiny as an atom, *anu*.

Mahima, the power of magnifying or making one's body or anything else *mahat*, as large as he likes.

Laghima, the power of making one's body or anything else *laghu*, as light in weight as he likes.

Garima, the power of making one's body or anything else *guru*, as heavy as he likes.

Prapti, the power of *apti*, obtaining anything he likes.

Vasitwa, the power of *vasa*, bringing anything under control.

Prakamya, the power of satisfying all desires, *kama*, by irresistible will force.

Isitxva, the power of becoming *Isa*, Lord, over everything. See John 14:12.

"Verily, verily, I say unto you, he that believeth on me, the works that I do shall he do also; and greater works than these shall he do; because I go unto my Father."

> SUTRA 12: "Knowledge of evolution, life, and dissolution thus leads to complete emancipation from the bonds of Maya, delusion. Beholding the self in the Supreme Self, man gains eternal freedom."

Thus man, being possessed of aiswaryas, the ascetic majesties aforesaid, fully comprehends the Eternal Spirit, the Father, the only Real Substance, as Unit, the Perfect Whole, and his Self as nothing but a mere idea resting on a fragment of the Spiritual Light thereof. Man, thus comprehending, abandons altogether the vain idea of the separate existence of his own Self and becomes unified with Him, the Eternal Spirit, God the Father. This unification with God is Kaivalya, the ultimate goal of man, as explained in this treatise. See Revelation 3:21.

"To him that overcometh will I grant to sit with me in my throne, even as I also overcame, and am set down with my Father in his throne."

CONCLUSION

"Love rules the court, the camp, the grove; The men below and saints above; For love is heaven and heaven is love." -Sir Walter Scott

The power of love has been beautifully described by the poet in the stanza quoted above. It has been clearly demonstrated in the foregoing pages that "Love is God," not merely as the noblest sentiment of a poet but as an aphorism of eternal truth. To whatever religious creed a man may belong and whatever may be his position in society, if he properly cultivates this ruling principle naturally implanted in his heart, he is sure to be on the right path, to save himself from wandering in this creation of Darkness, Maya.

It has been shown in the foregoing pages how love may be cultivated, how by its culture it attains development, and when developed, through this means only, how man may find his Spiritual Preceptor, through whose favor he again becomes baptized in the holy stream, and sacrifices his Self before the altar of God, becoming unified with the Eternal Father forever and ever. This little volume is therefore concluded with an earnest exhortation to the reader never to forget the great goal of life. In the words of the illumined sage, Sankaracharya:

"Life is always unsafe and unstable, like a drop of water on a lotus leaf. The company of a divine personage, even for a moment, can save and redeem us."

Made in the USA
Las Vegas, NV
19 March 2021